T0193673

The Broken Curse

The Broken Curse

Lyn Christian

THE BROKEN CURSE

iUniverse books may be ordered through booksellers or by contacting:

iUniverse
1663 Liberty Drive
Bloomington, IN 47403
www.iuniverse.com
1-800-Authors (1-800-288-4677)

Because of the dynamic nature of the Internet, any web addresses or links contained in this book may have changed since publication and may no longer be valid. The views expressed in this work are solely those of the author and do not necessarily reflect the views of the publisher, and the publisher hereby disclaims any responsibility for them.

Any people depicted in stock imagery provided by Thinkstock are models, and such images are being used for illustrative purposes only. Certain stock imagery © Thinkstock.

ISBN: 978-1-5320-1895-4 (sc)
ISBN: 978-1-5320-1896-1 (e)

Print information available on the last page.

iUniverse rev. date: 03/28/2017

The 45 Cub players that broke the curse are as follows:

Name	How Acquired
Albert Almora Jr (Right Handed Batter)	Drafted 1st Round #6 on 6-4-12
Jake Arrieta - (RHP)	Oriole trade on 7-20-13
Javier Baez - (RHB)	Drafted 1st Round #9 on 6-6-11
Kris Bryant (RHB)	Drafted 1st Round #2 on 6-6-13
Jake Buchanan (RHP)	Signed 3-31-16
Trevor Cahill (RHP)	Signed on 8-18-15
Jeimer Candelario (Switch Batter)	Signed 11-20-10
Aroldis Chapman (LHP)	Yankee trade on 7-25-16
Chris Coghlan (LHB)	Signed on 1-20-14
	Oakland trade on 2-25-16
	Oakland trade on 6-9-16
Gerald Concepcion (LHP)	Signed on 3-11-12
Wilson Contreras (LHB)	Signed on 7-15-09
Cul Edwards Jr. (RHP)	Rangers trade on 7-22-13
Tim Federowicz (RHB)	Signed 1-14-16
Dexter Fowler (Switch)	Astros trade on 1-19-15
Justin Grimm (RHP)	Ranger trade on 7-22-13
Jason Hammel (RHP)	Signed on 1-13-14
	Athletics trade on 7-4-14
	Signed 12-8-14
Kyle Hendricks (RHP)	Ranger trade on 7-31-12
Jason Heyward (LHB)	Signed 12-15-15
Ryan Kalish (LHP)	Signed 12-13-13
Munenori Kawasaki (LHB)	Signed 1-21-16
John Lackey (RHP)	Signed 12-8-15

Tommy La Stella (LHB)	Braves trade on 11-16-14
Jon Lester (LHP)	Signed 12-15-14
Brian Matusz (LHP)	Signed 6-15-16
Mike Montgomery (LHP)	Mariner trade on 7-20-16
Miguel Montero (LHB)	Diamond back trade on 12-9-14
Joe Nathan (RHP)	Signed 5-17-16
Spencer Patton (RHP)	Ranger trade on 11-20-15
Felix Pena (RHP)	Signed on 5-29-09
Joel Peralta (RHP)	Signed on 6-10-16
	Retired on 9-16-16
Neil Ramirez (RHP)	Signed on 8-23-13
Clayton Richard (LHP)	Pirate trade on 7-13-15
Anthony Rizzo (LHB)	Padre trade on 1-6-12
Hector Rondon (RHP)	Rule 5 from Athletics on 12-6-12
David Ross (RHB)	Signed 12-23-14
Addison Russell (RHB)	Athletics trade on 7-4-14
Kyle Schwarber (LHB)	Drafted Round 1 #4 on 6-5-14
Joe Smith (RHP)	Angel trade 8-1-16
Jorge Soler (RHB)	Signed 6-30-12
Pedro Strop (RHP)	Oriole trade on 7-20-13
Matt Szczur (RHB)	Drafted 5th Round #160 on 6-8-10
Adam Warren (RHP)	Yankee trade on 12-8-15
	Yankee trade on 7-25-16
Travis Wood (LHP)	Reds trade on 12-21-11
Rob Zastryzny (LHP)	Drafted 2nd Round #41 on 6-18-13
Ben Zobrist (Switch)	Signed 12-8-15

Acquasition of the 45 players in date order

5-29-09	Signed Felix Pena
7-15-09	Signed Wilson Contreras
6-8-10	Drafted Matt Szczur - 5th Round #160
11-20-10	Signed Jeimer Candelario
6-6-11	Drafted Javier Baez - 1st Round #9
12-12-11	Signed Theo Epstein as President of Baseball Operations
	" Jed Hoyer as General Manager
	" Jason McLeod as Player Development
12-21-11	Traded with Cincinnati for Travis Woods
1-6-12	Traded with San Diego for Anthony Rizzo
3-11-12	Signed Gerald Concepcion
6-4-12	Drafted Albert Almora Jr. - 1st Round #6
6-30-12	Signed Jorge Soler
7-31-12	Traded with Texas for Kyle Hendricks
12-6-12	Acquired Hector Rondon from Cleveland - Rule 5
6-6-13	Drafted Kris Bryant - 1st Round #2
6-18-13	Drafted Rob Zastryzny - 2nd Round #41
7-20-13	Traded with Baltimore for Jake Arrieta & Pedro Strop
7-22-13	Traded with Texas for Carl Edwards Jr. and Justin Grimm
8-23-13	Signed Neil Ramirez
12-13-13	Signed Ryan Kalish
1-13-14	Signed Jason Hammel
1-20-14	Signed Chris Coghlan
6-5-14	Drafted Kyle Schwarber - Round 1 #4
7-4-14	Traded Jason Hammel to Oakland for Addison Russell
11-2-14	Signed Joe Madden as Cub Manager
11-16-14	Traded with Atlanta for Tommy La Stella
12-8-14	Signed Jason Hammel
12-9-14	Traded with Arizona for Miguel Montero
12-15-14	Signed Jon Lester - 6 Years for $155 M

12-23-14	Signed David Ross
1-19-15	Traded with Houston for Dexter Fowler
7-13-15	Bought Clayton Richard from Pittsburgh
8-18-15	Signed Trevor Cahill
11-20-15	Traded with Texas for Spencer Patton
12-8-15	Signed John Lackey
	Traded with N.Y. Yankees for Adam Warren
	Signed Ben Zobrist - 4 Years - 56 M
12-12-15	Signed Jason Heyward - 8 Years - 184 M
1-14-16	Signed Tim Federowicz
1-21-16	Signed Munenori Kawasaki
2-25-16	Traded Chris Coghan to Oakland
3-31-16	Signed Jake Buchanan
5-17-16	Signed Joe Nathan
6-9-16	Traded with Oakland for Chris Coghlan
6-10-16	Signed Joel Peralta
6-15-16	Signed Brian Matusz
7-20-16	Traded with Seattle for Mike Montgomery
7-25-16	Traded Adam Warren to N.Y. Yankees for Aroldis Chapman
8-1-16	Traded with Los Angeles Angels for Joe Smith

Preseason Predictions for the World Series

<u>Las Vegas</u>

6-1	Chicago Cubs, S. F. Giants
9-1	Boston Red Sox
14-1	N. Y. Mets, K. C. Royals
16-1	L.A. Dodgers, Toronto Blue Jays, St. Louis Cardinals
18-1	Washington Nationals, Houston Astros, Pittsburgh Pirates
20-1	Texas Rangers, Arizona Diamondbacks
25-1	Cleveland Indians, L. A. Angels, N. Y. Yankees, Detroit Tigers
33-1	Seattle Mariners
50-1	Baltimore Orioles, Minnesota Twins, Chicago White Sox
66-1	Tampa Bay Rays, Miami Marlins
75-1	Milwaukee Brewers, Oakland Athletics
100-1	Cincinnati Reds, San Diego Padres, Atlanta Braves
	Colorado Rockies, Philadelphia Phillies

<u>Sports Illustrated</u>

Cubs to win the World Series

Cubs Opening Day Roster

13 Pitchers

Jake Arrieta, Trevor Cahill, Justin Grimm
Jason Hammel, Kyle Hendricks, John Lackey
Jon Lester, Neil Ramirez, Clayton Richard, Hector Rondon, Pedro Strop, Adam Warren, Travis Wood

2 Catchers

David Ross, Miguel Montero

5 Infielders

Kris Bryant, Tommy La Stella, Anthony Rizzo, Addison Russell, Ben Zobrist

5 Outfielders

Dexter Fowler, Jason Heyward, Kyle Schwarber, Jorge Soler, Matt Szczar

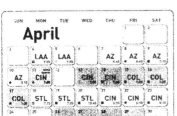

Changes Made During the Season

4-8-16	Placed Kyle Schwarber on the D. L. Called up Munenori Kawasaki
4-15-16	Called up Javier Baez to replace Munenori Kawasaki
4-29-16	Put Miguel Montero on the D. L. Called up Tim Federowicz
5-4-16	Placed Matt Szczar on the D. L. Called up Ryan Kalish
5-5-16	Placed Neil Ramirez on the bereavement list. Called up Spencer Patton.
5-8-16	Removed Neil Ramirez from the bereavement list. Sent Spencer Patton to minors.
5-11-16	Called up Carl Edwards Jr.
5-14-16	Called up Miguel Montero. Sent Ryan Kalish to minors
5-17-16	Signed Joe Nathan
5-21-16	Called up Matt Szczur. Sent Neil Ramirez to minors
6-7-16	Placed Jorge Soler on the D. L. Called up Albert Almora Jr.
6-9-16	Traded with Oakland for Chris Coghlan.
6-10-16	Called up Chris Coghlan. Put Tommy La Stella on the D. L.
6-13-16	Signed Joel Peralta
6-15-16	Signed Brian Matusz
6-18-16	Called up Wilson Contreras. Sent Tom Federowicz to the minors.
6-20-16	Put Dexter Fowler on the D. L. Called up Carl Edwards Jr.
7-4-16	Put Chris Coghlan on the D. L. Called up Jeimer Candelario
7-6-16	Placed David Ross on the D. L. Called up Adam Warren and Tommy La Stella. Sent Joel Peralta to the minors
7-10-16	Called up Munenori Kawasaki. Sent Jeimer Candelario to the minors
7-12-16	Sent Munenori Kawasaki to the minors
7-15-16	Put Trevor Cahill on the D. L. Called up David Ross and Clayton Richard
7-20-16	Traded with Seattle for Mike Montgomery

7-25-16	Sent Adam Warren to the N. Y. Yankees for Aroldis Chapman
7-29-16	Called up Chris Coghlan. Sent Tommy La Stella to the minors.
7-31-16	Sent Justin Grimm to the minors. Called up Brian Matusz
8-1-16	Traded with L. A. Angels for Joe Smith. Called up Spencer Patton. Sent Brian Matusz to the minors.
8-2-16	Sent Spencer Patton to the minors.
8-3-16	Put Jason Hammel on the bereavement list. Called up Justin Grimm
8-5-16	Called up Jorge Soler. Sent Joe Nathan to the minors.
8-9-16	Sent Justin Grimm to the minors. Took Jason Hammel off the bereavement list.
8-12-16	Put Pedro Strop on the D. L. Called up Justin Grimm
8-16-16	Called up Trevor Cahill
8-17-16	Called up Spencer Patton. Put Chris Coghlan on the D. L.
8-19-16	Put John Lackey and Hector Rondon on the D. L. Called up Felix Pena and Rob Zastryzny.
8-31-16	Called up Tommy La Stella. Sent Spencer Patton to the minors.
9-1-16	Called up Jake Buchanan, Chris Coghlan and Joe Smith
9-4-16	Called up John Lackey
9-6-16	Called up Hector Rondon, Spencer Patton, Albert Almora Jr. Munenori Kawasaki and Tim Federowicz
9-23-16	Called up Pedro Strop
9-28-16	Extended Theo Epstein contract for another 5 years
9-30-16	Extended Joel Hoyer and Jason McLeod contracts for another 5 years.

FINAL STANDINGS

October 2, 2016

East

	W	L	PCT	GB	L10	STRK	HOME	ROAD	LAST GAME	NEXT GAME
y-Boston Red Sox	93	69	.574	-	5-5	L2	47-34	46-35	10/2 vs TOR, L 1-2	10/6 @ CLE
w-Baltimore Orioles	89	73	.549	4.0	7-3	W1	50-31	39-42	10/2 @ NYY, W 5-2	10/4 @ TOR, 8:00 PM
w-Toronto Blue Jays	89	73	.549	4.0	6-4	W2	46-35	43-38	10/2 @ BOS, W 2-1	10/4 vs BAL, 8:00 PM
New York Yankees	84	78	.519	9.0	5-5	L1	48-33	36-45	10/2 vs BAL, L 2-5	--
Tampa Bay Rays	68	94	.420	25.0	3-7	W2	36-45	32-49	10/2 @ TEX, W 6-4	--

Central

	W	L	PCT	GB	L10	STRK	HOME	ROAD	LAST GAME	NEXT GAME
y-Cleveland Indians	94	67	.584	-	6-4	W3	53-28	41-39	10/2 @ KC, W 3-2	10/6 vs BOS
Detroit Tigers	86	75	.534	8.0	5-5	L2	45-35	41-40	10/2 @ ATL, L 0-1	--
Kansas City Royals	81	81	.500	13.5	4-6	L4	47-34	34-47	10/2 vs CLE, L 2-3	--
Chicago White Sox	78	84	.481	16.5	6-4	L2	45-36	33-48	10/2 vs MIN, L 3-6	--
Minnesota Twins	59	103	.364	35.5	4-6	W2	30-51	29-52	10/2 @ CWS, W 6-3	--

West

	W	L	PCT	GB	L10	STRK	HOME	ROAD	LAST GAME	NEXT GAME
z-Texas Rangers	95	67	.586	-	5-5	L2	53-28	42-39	10/2 vs TB, L 4-6	10/6 vs ALWC
Seattle Mariners	86	76	.531	9.0	6-4	L2	44-37	42-39	10/2 vs OAK, L 2-3	--
Houston Astros	84	78	.519	11.0	3-7	L1	43-38	41-40	10/2 @ LAA, L 1-8	--
Los Angeles Angels	74	88	.457	21.0	8-2	W1	40-41	34-47	10/2 vs HOU, W 8-1	--
Oakland Athletics	69	93	.426	26.0	3-7	W2	34-47	35-46	10/2 @ SEA, W 3-2	--

East

	W	L	PCT	GB	L10	STRK	HOME	ROAD	LAST GAME	NEXT GAME
y-Washington Nationals	95	67	.586	-	6-4	W2	50-31	45-36	10/2 vs MIA, W 10-7	10/7 vs LAD
w-New York Mets	87	75	.537	8.0	7-3	L1	44-37	43-38	10/2 @ PHI, L 2-5	10/5 vs SF, 8:00 PM

	W	L	PCT	GB	L10	STRK	HOME	ROAD	LAST GAME	NEXT GAME
Miami Marlins	79	82	.491	15.5	3-7	L2	40-40	39-42	10/2 @ WSH, L 7-10	--
Philadelphia Phillies	71	91	.438	24.0	2-8	W1	37-44	34-47	10/2 vs NYM, W 5-2	--
Atlanta Braves	68	93	.422	26.5	8-2	W2	31-50	37-43	10/2 vs DET, W 1-0	--
Central	**W**	**L**	**PCT**	**GB**	**L10**	**STRK**	**HOME**	**ROAD**	**LAST GAME**	**NEXT GAME**
z-Chicago Cubs	103	58	.640	-	7-3	W1	57-24	46-34	10/2 @ CIN, W 7-4	10/7 vs NLWC
St. Louis Cardinals	86	76	.531	17.5	6-4	W4	38-43	48-33	10/2 vs PIT, W 10-4	--
Pittsburgh Pirates	78	83	.484	25.0	2-8	L3	38-42	40-41	10/2 @ STL, L 4-10	--
Milwaukee Brewers	73	89	.451	30.5	5-5	W2	41-40	32-49	10/2 @ COL, W 6-4	--
Cincinnati Reds	68	94	.420	35.5	5-5	L1	38-43	30-51	10/2 vs CHC, L 4-7	--
West	**W**	**L**	**PCT**	**GB**	**L10**	**STRK**	**HOME**	**ROAD**	**LAST GAME**	**NEXT GAME**
y-Los Angeles Dodgers	91	71	.562	-	5-5	L3	53-28	38-43	10/2 @ SF, L 1-7	10/7 @ WSH
w-San Francisco Giants	87	75	.537	4.0	7-3	W4	45-36	42-39	10/2 vs LAD, W 7-1	10/5 @ NYM 8:00 PM
Colorado Rockies	75	87	.463	16.0	2-8	L2	42-39	33-48	10/2 vs MIL, L 4-6	--
Arizona Diamondbacks	69	93	.426	22.0	5-5	W3	33-48	36-45	10/2 vs SD, W 3-2	--
San Diego Padres	68	94	.420	23.0	4-6	L4	39-42	29-52	10/2 @ ARI, L 2-3	--

w - clinched wild card

x - clinched playoff berth

y - clinched division

z - clinched division and best record in league

Tie Games

September 28, Cubs 1 at Pirates 1

Tie games do not count towards standings calculations

The Results of 2016 season

Date	Opponent	Result	Record	Winning Pitcher	Losing Pitcher
Mon, 4/4	at Angels	W 9-0	1-0	Arrieta(1-0)	Richards(0-1)
Tue, 4/5	at Angels	W 6-1	2-0	Lester(1-0)	Heaney(0-1)
Thu, 4/7	at D-backs	W 14-6	3-0	Lackey(1-0)	De La Rosa(0-1)
Fri, 4/8	at D-backs	L 2-3	3-1	Ziegler(1-0)	Cahill(0-1)
Sat, 4/9	at D-backs	W 4-2	4-1	Hendricks(1-0)	Greinke(0-2)
Sun, 4/10	at D-backs	W 7-3	5-1	Arrieta(2-0)	Miller(0-1)
Mon, 4/11	Reds	W 5-3	6-1	Warren(1-0)	Cingrani(0-1)
Wed, 4/13	Reds	W 9-2	7-1	Lackey(2-0)	Simon(0-1)
Thu, 4/14	Reds	W 8-1	8-1	Hammel(1-0)	Iglesias(1-1)
Fri, 4/15	Rockies	L 1-6	8-2	Bettis(2-0)	Hendricks(1-1)
Sat, 4/16	Rockies	W 6-2	9-2	Arrieta(3-0)	Bergman(0-2)
Sun, 4/17	Rockies	L 0-2	9-3	Chatwood(2-1)	Lester(1-1)
Mon, 4/18	at Cardinals	W 5-0	10-3	Lackey(3-0)	Leake(0-2)
Tue, 4/19	at Cardinals	W 2-1	11-3	Hammel(2-0)	Garcia(1-1)
Wed, 4/20	at Cardinals	L 3-5	11-4	Martinez(3-0)	Hendricks(1-2)
Thu, 4/21	at Reds	W 16-0	12-4	Arrieta(4-0)	Finnegan(1-1)
Fri, 4/22	at Reds	W 8-1	13-4	Lester(2-1)	Moscot(0-1)
Sat, 4/23	at Reds	L 5-13	13-5	Wood(2-0)	Lackey(3-1)
Sun, 4/24	at Reds	W 9-0	14-5	Hammel(3-0)	Simon(0-2)
Tue, 4/26	Brewers	W 4-3	15-5	Warren(2-0)	Nelson(3-2)
Wed, 4/27	Brewers	Postponed	15-5	Cahill(0-1)	Garza(0-0)
Thu, 4/28	Brewers	W 7-2	16-5	Arrieta(5-0)	Jungmann(0-4)
Fri, 4/29	Braves	W 6-1	17-5	Strop(1-0)	Johnson(0-3)

Sat, 4/30	Braves	Postponed	17-5	Alvarez(0-0)	Patton(0-0)
Sun, 5/1	Braves	L 3-4	17-6	Vizcaino(1-0)	Rondon(0-1)
Mon, 5/2	at Pirates	W 7-2	18-6	Hammel(4-0)	Cole(2-3)
Tue, 5/3	at Pirates	W 7-1	19-6	Arrieta(6-0)	Niese(3-1)
Wed, 5/4	at Pirates	W 6-2	20-6	Lester(3-1)	Nicasio(3-3)
Thu, 5/5	Nationals	W 5-2	21-6	Hendricks(2-2)	Ross(3-1)
Fri, 5/6	Nationals	W 8-6	22-6	Lackey(4-1)	Scherzer(3-2)
Sat, 5/7	Nationals	W 8-5	23-6	Warren(3-0)	Solis(0-1)
Sun, 5/8	Nationals	W 4-3	24-6	Wood(1-0)	Treinen(2-1)
Mon, 5/9	Padres	Postponed	24-6	Villanueva(0-0)	Strop(1-0)
Tue, 5/10	Padres	W 8-7	25-6	Lester(4-1)	Vargas(0-2)
Wed, 5/11	Padres	L 4-7	25-7	Villanueva(1-0)	Strop(1-1)
Wed, 5/11	Padres	L 0-1	25-8	Pomeranz(4-3)	Lackey(4-2)
Fri, 5/13	Pirates	W 9-4	26-8	Hammel(5-0)	Liriano(3-2)
Sat, 5/14	Pirates	W 8-2	27-8	Arrieta(7-0)	Lockey(1-3)
Sun, 5/15	Pirates	L 1-2	27-9	Cole(4-3)	Lester(4-2)
Tue, 5/17	at Brewers	L 2-4	27-10	Anderson(2-5)	Hendricks(2-3)
Wed, 5/18	at Brewers	W 2-1	28-10	Wood(2-0)	Torres(0-1)
Thu, 5/19	at Brewers	L 3-5	28-11	Guerra(3-0)	Hammel(5-1)
Fri, 5/20	at Giants	W 8-1	29-11	Arrieta(8-0)	Peavy(1-5)
Sat, 5/21	at Giants	L 3-5	29-12	Cain(1-5)	Lester(4-3)
Sun, 5/22	at Giants	L 0-1	29-13	Bumgarner(6-2)	Hendricks(2-4)
Mon, 5/23	at Cardinals	L 3-4	29-14	Rosenthal(2-1)	Warren(3-1)
Tue, 5/24	at Cardinals	W 12-3	30-14	Hammel(6-1)	Wacha(2-5)
Wed, 5/25	at Cardinals	W 9-8	31-14	Arrieta(9-0)	Martinez(4-5)
Fri, 5/27	Phillies	W 6-2	32-14	Lester(5-3)	Morgan(1-3)

Sat, 5/28	Phillies	W 4-1	33-14	Hendricks(3-4)	Eickhoff(2-7)
Sun, 5/29	Phillies	W 7-2	34-14	Lackey(5-2)	Velasquez(5-2)
Mon, 5/30	Dodgers	W 2-0	35-14	Wood(3-0)	Wood(1-4)
Tue, 5/31	Dodgers	L 0-5	35-15	Blanton(3-2)	Richard(0-1)
Wed, 6/1	Dodgers	W 2-1	36-15	Lester(6-3)	Bolsinger(1-2)
Thu, 6/2	Dodgers	W 7-2	37-15	Hendricks(4-4)	Urias(0-1)
Fri, 6/3	D-backs	W 6-0	38-15	Lackey(6-2)	Bradley(2-1)
Sat, 6/4	D-backs	W 5-3	39-15	Hammel(7-1)	Escobar(0-2)
Sun, 6/5	D-backs	L 2-3	39-16	Corbin(3-5)	Arrieta(9-1)
Mon, 6/6	at Phillies	W 6-4	40-16	Lester(7-3)	Morgan(1-5)
Tue, 6/7	at Phillies	L 2-3	40-17	Eickhoff(3-8)	Hendricks(4-5)
Wed, 6/8	at Phillies	W 8-1	41-17	Lackey(7-2)	Oberholtzer(2-1)
Fri, 6/10	at Braves	L 1-5	41-18	Norris(2-7)	Hammel(7-2)
Sat, 6/11	at Braves	W 8-2	42-18	Arrieta(10-1)	Wisler(2-7)
Sun, 6/12	at Braves	W 13-2	43-18	Lester(8-3)	Gant(0-1)
Mon, 6/13	at Nationals	L 1-4	43-19	Scherzer(8-4)	Hendricks(4-6)
Tue, 6/14	at Nationals	W 4-3	44-19	Rondon(1-1)	Solis(1-2)
Wed, 6/15	at Nationals	L 4-5	44-20	Petit(2-0)	Cahill(0-2)
Fri, 6/17	Pirates	W 6-0	45-20	Arrieta(11-1)	Liriano(4-7)
Sat, 6/18	Pirates	W 4-3	46-20	Lester(9-3)	Niese(6-4)
Sun, 6/19	Pirates	W 10-5	47-20	Hendricks(5-6)	Taillon(1-1)
Mon, 6/20	Cardinals	L 2-3	47-21	Garcia(5-6)	Lackey(7-3)
Tue, 6/21	Cardinals	L 3-4	47-22	Wainwright(6-4)	Hammel(7-3)
Wed, 6/22	Cardinals	L 2-7	47-23	Wacha(3-7)	Arrieta(11-2)
Thu, 6/23	at Marlins	L 2-4	47-24	Barraclough(4-2)	Strop(1-2)
Fri, 6/24	at Marlins	W 5-4	48-24	Cahill(1-2)	Dunn(0-1)

Date	Opponent	Result	Record	Winning Pitcher	Losing Pitcher
Sat, 6/25	at Marlins	L 6-9	48-25	Clemens(1-0)	Lackey(7-4)
Sun, 6/26	at Marlins	L 1-6	48-26	Fernandez(10-3)	Hammel(7-4)
Mon, 6/27	at Reds	W 11-8	49-26	Arrieta(12-2)	Straily(4-5)
Tue, 6/28	at Reds	W 7-2	50-26	Patton(1-0)	Hoover(1-2)
Wed, 6/29	at Reds	W 9-2	51-26	Hendricks(6-6)	Reed(0-2)
Thu, 6/30	at Mets	L 3-4	51-27	Goeddel(1-0)	Peralta(0-1)
Fri, 7/1	at Mets	L 2-10	51-28	deGrom(4-4)	Hammel(7-5)
Sat, 7/2	at Mets	L 3-4	51-29	Colon(7-4)	Arrieta(12-3)
Sun, 7/3	at Mets	L 3-14	51-30	Syndergaard(9-3)	Lester(9-4)
Mon, 7/4	Reds	W 10-4	52-30	Hendricks(7-6)	Reed(0-3)
Tue, 7/5	Reds	L 5-9	52-31	Finnegan(4-7)	Lackey(7-5)
Wed, 7/6	Reds	L 3-5	52-32	DeSclafani(3-0)	Cahill(1-3)
Thu, 7/7	Braves	L 3-4	52-33	Alvarez(3-1)	Patton(1-1)
Fri, 7/8	at Pirates	L 4-8	52-34	Feliz(3-0)	Arrieta(12-4)
Sat, 7/9	at Pirates	L 6-12	52-35	Caminero(1-2)	Warren(3-2)
Sun, 7/10	at Pirates	W 6-5	53-35	Strop(2-2)	Watson(1-3)
Fri, 7/15	Rangers	W 6-0	54-35	Hendricks(8-6)	Perez(7-6)
Sat, 7/16	Rangers	W 3-1	55-35	Hammel(8-5)	Darvish(2-1)
Sun, 7/17	Rangers	L 1-4	55-36	Hamels(10-2)	Lackey(7-6)
Mon, 7/18	Mets	W 5-1	56-36	Lester(10-4)	Matz(7-6)
Tue, 7/19	Mets	L 1-2	56-37	Robles(4-3)	Rondon(1-2)
Wed, 7/20	Mets	W 6-2	57-37	Hendricks(9-6)	Colon(8-5)
Fri, 7/22	at Brewers	W 5-2	58-37	Hammel(9-5)	Nelson(6-8)
Sat, 7/23	at Brewers	L 1-6	58-38	Davies(7-4)	Lackey(7-7)
Sun, 7/24	at Brewers	W 6-5	59-38	Nathan(1-0)	Smith(1-3)

Date	Opponent	Result	Record		
Mon, 7/25	at White Sox	L 4-5	59-39	Jennings(4-2)	Montgomery(0-1)
Tue, 7/26	at White Sox	L 0-3	59-40	Shields(3-5)	Hendricks(9-7)
Wed, 7/27	White Sox	W 8-1	60-40	Hammel(10-5)	Ranaudo(0-1)
Thu, 7/28	White Sox	W 3-1	61-40	Lackey(8-7)	Sale(14-4)
Fri, 7/29	Mariners	W 12-1	62-40	Lester(11-4)	Iwakuma(11-7)
Sat, 7/30	Mariners	L 1-4	62-41	Miley(7-8)	Arrieta(12-5)
Sun, 7/31	Mariners	W 7-6	63-41	Rondon(2-2)	Martin(1-1)
Mon, 8/1	Marlins	W 5-0	64-41	Hendricks(10-7)	Conley(7-6)
Tue, 8/2	Marlins	W 3-2	65-41	Hammel(11-5)	Fernandez(12-6)
Wed, 8/3	Marlins	W 5-4	66-41	Grimm(1-0)	Ramos(1-1)
Fri, 8/5	at Athletics	W 7-2	67-41	Lester(12-4)	Overton(1-3)
Sat, 8/6	at Athletics	W 4-0	68-41	Arrieta(13-5)	Gray(5-11)
Sun, 8/7	at Athletics	W 3-1	69-41	Hendricks(11-7)	Manaea(3-7)
Tue, 8/9	Angels	W 5-1	70-41	Lackey(9-7)	Weaver(8-9)
Wed, 8/10	Angels	W 3-1	71-41	Hammel(12-5)	Nolasco(0-1)
Thu, 8/11	Cardinals	W 4-3	72-41	Montgomery(1-1)	Duke(0-1)
Fri, 8/12	Cardinals	W 13-2	73-41	Arrieta(14-5)	Wainwright(9-7)
Sat, 8/13	Cardinals	L 4-8	73-42	Reyes(1-0)	Edwards Jr.(0-1)
Sun, 8/14	Cardinals	L 4-6	73-43	Bowman(2-4)	Rondon(2-3)
Tue, 8/16	Brewers	W 4-0	74-43	Cahill(2-3)	Garza(4-5)
Tue, 8/16	Brewers	W 4-1	75-43	Hammel(13-5)	Marinez(0-1)
Wed, 8/17	Brewers	W 6-1	76-43	Lester(13-4)	Nelson(6-13)
Thu, 8/18	Brewers	W 9-6	77-43	Arrieta(15-5)	Davies(9-6)
Fri, 8/19	at Rockies	L 6-7	77-44	Carasiti(1-0)	Chapman(0-1)
Sat, 8/20	at Rockies	W 9-2	78-44	Cahill(3-3)	Hoffman(0-1)
Sun, 8/21	at Rockies	L 4-11	78-45	De La Rosa(8-7)	Hammel(13-6)

Date	Opponent	Result	Record	Pitcher	Pitcher
Mon, 8/22	at Padres	W 5-1	79-45	Lester(14-4)	Jackson(3-3)
Tue, 8/23	at Padres	W 5-3	80-45	Arrieta(16-5)	Friedrich(4-10)
Wed, 8/24	at Padres	W 6-3	81-45	Hendricks(12-7)	Clemens(1-3)
Fri, 8/26	at Dodgers	W 6-4	82-45	Wood(4-0)	Liberatore(2-1)
Sat, 8/27	at Dodgers	L 2-3	82-46	Urias(5-2)	Hammel(13-7)
Sun, 8/28	at Dodgers	L 0-1	82-47	Blanton(5-2)	Cahill(3-4)
Mon, 8/29	Pirates	W 8-7	83-47	Zastryzny(1-0)	Locke(9-8)
Tue, 8/30	Pirates	W 3-0	84-47	Hendricks(13-7)	Kuhl(3-2)
Wed, 8/31	Pirates	W 6-5	85-47	Hammel(14-7)	Vogelsong(3-4)
Thu, 9/1	Giants	W 5-4	86-47	Smith(1-0)	Strickland(3-2)
Fri, 9/2	Giants	W 2-1	87-47	Lester(15-4)	Suarez(3-3)
Sat, 9/3	Giants	L 2-3	87-48	Bumgarner(14-8)	Arrieta(16-6)
Sun, 9/4	Giants	W 3-2	88-48	Cahill(4-4)	Reynolds(0-1)
Mon, 9/5	at Brewers	W 7-2	89-48	Hendricks(14-7)	Davies(10-7)
Tue, 9/6	at Brewers	L 5-12	89-49	Peralta(6-9)	Hammel(14-8)
Wed, 9/7	at Brewers	L 1-2	89-50	Knebel(1-2)	Smith(1-1)
Fri, 9/9	at Astros	W 2-0	90-50	Lester(16-4)	Musgrove(2-4)
Sat, 9/10	at Astros	L 1-2	90-51	McHugh(10-10)	Lackey(9-8)
Sun, 9/11	at Astros	W 9-5	91-51	Arrieta(17-6)	Fiers(10-7)
Mon, 9/12	at Cardinals	W 4-1	92-51	Hendricks(15-7)	Leake(9-10)
Tue, 9/13	at Cardinals	L 2-4	92-52	Reyes(2-1)	Hammel(14-9)
Wed, 9/14	at Cardinals	W 7-0	93-52	Lester(17-4)	Martinez(14-8)
Thu, 9/15	Brewers	L 4-5	93-53	Nelson(8-14)	Grimm(1-1)
Fri, 9/16	Brewers	W 5-4	94-53	Chapman(1-1)	Boyer(2-4)
Sat, 9/17	Brewers	L 3-11	94-54	Davies(11-7)	Arrieta(17-7)
Sun, 9/18	Brewers	L 1-3	94-55	Peralta(7-10)	Hendricks(15-8)

Date	Opponent	Result	Record	Winning Pitcher	Losing Pitcher
Mon, 9/19	Reds	W 5-2	95-55	Hammel(15-9)	Wood(6-4)
Tue, 9/20	Reds	W 6-1	96-55	Lester(18-4)	Smith(3-2)
Wed, 9/21	Reds	W 9-2	97-55	Lackey(10-8)	Stephenson(2-2)
Fri, 9/23	Cardinals	W 5-0	98-55	Arrieta(18-7)	Leake(9-11)
Sat, 9/24	Cardinals	L 4-10	98-56	Reyes(4-1)	Hammel(15-10)
Sun, 9/25	Cardinals	W 3-1	99-56	Lester(19-4)	Martinez(15-9)
Mon, 9/26	at Pirates	W 12-2	100-56	Hendricks(16-8)	Kuhl(5-4)
Tue, 9/27	at Pirates	W 6-4	101-56	Lackey(11-8)	Vogelsong(3-7)
Wed, 9/28	at Pirates	L 4-8	101-57	Taillon(5-4)	Arrieta(18-8)
Thu, 9/29	at Pirates	T 1-1	101-57		
Fri, 9/30	at Reds	W 7-3	102-57	Buchanan(1-0)	Smith(3-3)
Sat, 10/1	at Reds	L 4-7	102-58	Adleman(4-4)	Lester(19-5)
Sun, 10/2	at Reds	W 7-4	103-58	Grimm(2-1)	Iglesias(3-2)
Fri, 10/7	Giants	W 1-0	1-0	Lester(1-0)	Cueto(0-1)
Sat, 10/8	Giants	W 5-2	2-0	Wood(1-0)	Samardzija(0-1)
Mon, 10/10	at Giants	L 5-6	2-1	Blach(1-0)	Montgomery(0-1)
Tue, 10/11	at Giants	W 6-5	3-1	Rondon(1-0)	Smith(0-1)
Sat, 10/15	Dodgers	W 8-4	1-0	Chapman(1-0)	Blanton(0-1)
Sun, 10/16	Dodgers	L 0-1	1-1	Kershaw(1-0)	Hendricks(0-1)
Tue, 10/18	at Dodgers	L 0-6	1-2	Hill(1-0)	Arrieta(0-1)
Wed, 10/19	at Dodgers	W 10-2	2-2	Montgomery(1-0)	Urias(0-1)
Thu, 10/20	at Dodgers	W 8-4	3-2	Lester(1-0)	Blanton(0-2)
Sat, 10/22	Dodgers	W 5-0	4-2	Hendricks(1-1)	Kershaw(1-1)
Tue, 10/25	at Indians	L 0-6	0-1	Kluber(1-0)	Lester(0-1)
Wed, 10/26	at Indians	W 5-1	1-1	Arrieta(1-0)	Bauer(0-1)

Fri, 10/28	Indians	L 0-1	1-2	Miller(1-0)	Edwards Jr.(0-1)
Sat, 10/29	Indians	L 2-7	1-3	Kluber(2-0)	Lackey(0-1)
Sun, 10/30	Indians	W 3-2	2-3	Lester(1-1)	Bauer(0-2)
Tue, 11/1	at Indians	W 9-3	3-3	Arrieta(2-0)	Tomlin(0-1)
Wed, 11/2	at Indians	W 8-7	4-3	Chapman(1-0)	Shaw(0-1)

How The Cubs did against opposing teams they played

Arizona Diamondbacks	W-5	L-2	
Atlanta Braves	W-3	L-3	
Chicago White Sox	W-2	L-2	
Cincinnati Reds	W-15	L-4	
Colorado Rockies	W-2	L-4	
Houston Astros	W-2	L-1	
Los Angeles Angels	W-4	L-0	
Los Angeles Dodgers	W-4	L-3	
Miami Marlins	W-4	L-3	
Milwaukee Brewers	W-11	L-8	
New York Mets	W-2	L-5	
Oakland Athletics	W-3	L-0	
Philadelphia Phillies	W-5	L-1	
Pittsburgh Pirates	W-14	L-1	Tied-1
San Diego Padres	W-4	L-2	
San Francisco Giants	W-4	L-3	
Seattle Mariners	W-2	L-1	
St. Louis Cardinals	W-10	L-9	
Texas Rangers	W-2	L-1	
Washington Nationals	W-5	L-2	

One Run Games

4-8 (A)	D'Backs 3	Cubs 2
4-19 (A)	Cubs 2	Cardinals 1
4-26 (H)	Cubs 4	Brewers 3
5-1 (H)	Braves 4	Cubs 3
5-8 (H)	Cubs 4	Nationals 3 (13 inn)
5-10 (H)	Cubs 8	Padres 7
5-11 (H)	Padres 1	Cubs 0 2nd game
5-15 (H)	Pirates 2	Cubs 1
5-18 (A)	Cubs 2	Braves 1
5-22 (A)	Giants 1	Cubs 0
5-23 (A)	Cardinals 4	Cubs 3
5-25 (A)	Cubs 9	Cardinals 8
6-1 (H)	Cubs 2	Dodgers 1
6-5 (H)	D'Backs 3	Cubs 2
6-7 (A)	Phillies 3	Cubs 2
6-14 (A)	Cubs 4	Nationals 3
6-15 (A)	Nationals 5	Cubs 4
6-18 (H)	Cubs 4	Pirates 3
6-20 (H)	Cardinals 3	Cubs 2
6-21 (H)	Cardinals 4	Cubs 3
6-24 (A)	Cubs 5	Marlins 4
6-30 (A)	Mets 4	Cubs 3
7-2 (A)	Mets 4	Cubs 3
7-7 (H)	Brewers 4	Cubs 3
7-10 (A)	Cubs 6	Pirates 5
7-19 (H)	Mets 2	Cubs 1
7-24 (A)	Cubs 6	Brewers 5
7-25 (A)	W. Sox 5	Cubs 4
7-31 (H)	Cubs 7	Mariners 6 (12 inn)
8-2 (H)	Cubs 3	Marlins 2

8-3 (H)	Cubs 5	Martins 4
8-11 (H)	Cubs 4	Cardinals 3 (11 inn)
8-19 (A)	Rockies 7	Cubs 6 (11 inn)
8-27 (A)	Dodgers 3	Cubs 2
8-28 (A)	Dodgers 1	Cubs 0
8-29 (H)	Cubs 8	Pirates 7 (13 inn)
8-31 (H)	Cubs 6	Pirates 5
9-1 (H)	Cubs 5	Giants 4
9-2 (H)	Cubs 2	Giants 1
9-3 (H)	Giants 3	Cubs 2
9-4 (H)	Cubs 3	Giants 2 (13 inn)
9-7 (A)	Brewers	2 Cubs 1
9-10 (A)	Astros 2	Cubs 1
9-15 (H)	Brewers 5	Cubs 4
9-16 (H)	Cubs 5	Brewers 4

The Cubs won 22 and lost 23 of these games.

3 or More Consectutive Wins

4-4, 4-5, 4-7 | 4-9, 4-10, 4-11, 4-13, 4-14 | 4-24, 4-26, 4-28, 4-29 | 5-2, 5-3 5-4, 5-5, 5-6, 5-7, 5-8, 5-10 | 5-24, 5-25, 5-27, 5-28, 5-29, 5-30 | 6-1, 6-2, 6-3, 6-4 | 6-17, 6-18, 6-19 | 6-27, 6-28, 6-29 | 7-10, 7-15, 7-16 | 7-27, 7-28, 7-29 | 7-31, 8-1, 8-2, 8-3, 8-5, 8-6, 8-7, 8-9, 8-10, 8-11, 8-12 | 8-16, 8-16, 8-17, 8-18 | 8-22, 8-23, 8-24, 8-26 | 8-29, 8-30, 8-31, 9-1, 9-2 | 9-19 9-20, 9-21, 9-23 | 9-25, 9-26, 9-27

3 or More Consectutive Losses

5-21, 5-22, 5-23 | 6-20, 6-21, 6-22, 6-23 | 6-30, 7-1, 7-2, 7-3 | 7-5, 7-6, 7-7, 7-8, 7-9

Extra Inning Games

5-1 (H)	Braves 4	Cubs 3	10 Innings
5-8 (H)	Cubs 4	Nationals 3	13 "
5-18 (A)	Cubs 2	Brewers 1	13 "
6-15 (A)	Nationals 5	Cubs 4	12 "
6-28 (A)	Cubs 7	Reds 2	15 "
7-7 (H)	Braves 4	Cubs 3	11 "
7-31 (H)	Cubs 7	Mariners 6	12 "
8-11 (H)	Cubs 4	Cardinals 3	11 "
8-19 (A)	Rockies 7	Cubs 6	11 "
8-26 (A)	Cubs 6	Dodgers 4	10 "
8-29 (H)	Cubs 8	Pirates 7	13 "
9-4 (H)	Cubs 3	Giants 2	13 "
9-16 (H)	Cubs 5	Brewers 4	10 "

Shutout by and against the Cubs

4-4 (A)	Cubs 9 Angles 0	Arrieta - 7 innings, Grimm 1 inning, Wood 1 inning
4-17 (H)	Rockies 2 Cubs 0	Chatwood - 7 inn, Castio 1 inn. McGee 1 inn.
4-18 (A)	Cubs 5 Cardinals 0	Lackey - 7 inn, Wood ⅔ inn Strop ⅓ inn. Cahill 1 inn
4-22 (A)	Cubs 16 Reds 0	Arrieta's no hitter
4-24 (A)	Cubs 9 Reds 0	Hammel - 6 inn, Warren 1 inn, Wood 1 inn. Rondon 1 inn.

2ⁿᵈ Game

5-11 (H)	Padres 1 Cubs 0	Pomerang 6 inn, Quackenbush 1 inn Hand 1 inn Rodney 1 inn
5-22 (A)	Giants 1 Cubs 0	Bumgarner 7 ⅔ inn. Gearrin ⅓ inn. Carilla 1 inn.
5-30 (H)	Cubs 2 Dodgers 0	Hammel 2 inn, Wood 4 inn, Grimm 1 inn, Strop 1 inn, Rondon 1inn
5-31 (H)	Dodgers 5 Cubs 0	Kazmir 6 inn, Blanton 2 inn Liberatore 1 inn.
6-3 (H)	Cubs 6 D'Backs 0	Lackey 6⅔ inn. Warren ⅓ inn. Strop 1 inn Grimm 1 inn
6-17 (H)	Cubs 6 Pirates 0	Arrieta 6 inn. Cahill 1⅓ inn. Wood ⅔ inn. Grimm 1 inn
7-15 (H)	Cubs 6 Rangers 0	Hendricks 6 inn. Edwards 1 inn. Wood ⅔ inn. Strop ⅓ inn Grimm 1 inn.
7-26 (A)	White Sox 3 Cubs 0	Shields 7⅔ inn Jones ⅓ inn. Robertson 1 inn.
8-1 (H)	Cubs 5 Marlins 0	Hendricks 9 inn.
8-6 (A)	Cubs 4 Athletics 0	Arrieta 8 inn. Wood 1 inn.

1st Game

8-16 (H)	Cubs 4 Brewers 0	Cahill 5 inn. Montgomery 2 inn. Rondon 1 inn. Smith ⅓ inn Chapman ⅔ inn.
8-28 (A)	Dodgers 1 Cubs 0	Stewart 5 inn. Chavez ⅔ inn Dayton 1⅓ inn. Blanton 1 inn. Jansen 1 inn
8-30 (H)	Cubs 3 Pirates 0	Hendricks 7 inn. Edwards Jr. 1 inn, Chapman 1 inn
9-9 (A)	Cubs 2 Astros 0	Lester 7 inn. Rondon 1 inn. Chapman 1 inn.
9-14 (A)	Cubs 7 Cardinals 0	Lester 8 inn. Rondon 1 inn
9-23 (H)	Cubs 5 Cardinals 0	Arrieta 7 inn. Strop 1 inn. Wood ⅓ inn. Edwards Jr. ⅔ inn

Games where 1 team got 3 or less hits
* Pitchers on the losing team allowed 3 or less hits

4-4 (A)	Cubs 9 Angels 0	Arrieta - 2 Hits - 7 inning, Grimm 1 Hit 1 Inn Wood 0 Hits 1 inn.
4-11 (H) *	Cubs 5 Reds 3	Finnegan 1 Hit 6⅔ inn, Cothran 0 Hits - 0 inn. Cingrani 1 Hit ⅔ inn, Diaz 1 Hit ⅔ inn
4-17 (H)	Rockies 2 Cubs 0	Chatwood 2 Hits 7 inn Castro 0 Hit 1 inn. McGee 1 Hit 1 inn.
4-22 (A)	Cubs 16 Reds 0	Arrieta No Hit Game
4-24 (A)	Cubs 9 Reds 0	Hammel 3 Hits 6 inn. Warren 0 Hits 1 inn Wood 0 Hits 1 inn, Rondon 0 Hits 1 inn.(0 Hits)
5-3 (A)	Cubs 7 Pirates 1	Arrieta 2 Hits 7 inn, Cahill 1 Hit 2 inn
5-5 (H)	Cubs 5 Nationals 2	Hendricks 2 Hits 6 inn, Richard 0 Hits ⅓ inn Grimm 0 Hits ⅔ inn Strop 0 Hits 1 inn Wood 1 Hit ⅔ inn Rondon 0 Hits ⅓ inn

2nd Game

5-11 (H) *	Padres 1 Cubs 0	Lackey 3 Hits 8 inn, Wood 0 Hits ⅓ inn Rondon 0 Hits ⅔ inn.
5-14 (H)	Cubs 8 Pirates 2	Arrieta 3 Hits 8 inn. Grimm 0 Hits 1 inn.
5-17 (A)	Brewers 4 Cubs 2	Anderson 3 Hits ⅔ inn Jeffers 0 Hits ⅓ inn
5-22 (A)	Giants 1 Cubs 0	Baumgarner 3 Hits - 7⅔ inn, Gearrin 0 Hits ⅓ inn Casilla 0 Hits 1 inn
5-30 (H)	Cubs 2 Dodgers 0	Hammel 1 Hit 2 inn, Wood 0 Hits 4 inn, Grimm 0 Hit 1 inn, Strop 0 Hits 1 inn, Rondon 0 Hits 1 inn

(1 Hit)

27

5-31 (H)	Dodgers 5 Cubs 0	Kazmur 1 Hit 6 inn, Blanton 0 Hits 2 inn Liberatore 0 Hits 1 inn
6-1 (H) *	Cubs 2 Dodgers 1	Bolsinger 2 Hits 5 inn. Baez 0 Hits 2 inn Fien 1 Hit 1 inn
6-2 (H)	Cubs 7 Dodgers 2	Hendricks 3 Hits 8 inn, Wood 0 Hits 1 inn
6-8 (A)	Cubs 8 Phillies 1	Lackey 3 Hits 7 inn, Strop 0 Hits 1 inn Richard 0 Hits 1 inn.

(2 Hits)

6-13 (A)	National 4 Cubs 1	Schiezer 2 Hits 7 inn Perez 0 Hits $\frac{1}{3}$ inn Kelley 0 Hits 1$\frac{2}{3}$ inn
6-17 (H)	Cubs 6 Pirates 0	Arrieta 2 Hits 6 inn, Cahill 0 Hits 1$\frac{1}{3}$ inn, Wood 0 Hits $\frac{2}{3}$ inn Grimm 1 Hit 1 inn
6-22 (H)	Cards 7 Cubs 2	Wacka 3 Hits 6$\frac{2}{3}$ inn, Maness 0 Hits $\frac{2}{3}$ inn Lyons 0 Hits 1 inn Broxton 0 Hits $\frac{2}{3}$ inn

(2 Hits)

6-24 (H)	Cubs 5 Marlins 4	Hendricks 1 Hit 5 inn, Cahill 1 Hit 1 inn Wood 0 Hits 1$\frac{2}{3}$ inn, Rondon 0 Hits 1$\frac{1}{3}$ inn
7-16 (H)	Cubs 3 Rangers 1	Hammel 3 Hits 6 inn, Warren 0 Hits $\frac{2}{3}$ inn Wood 0 Hits 1$\frac{1}{3}$ inn, Rondon 0 Hits 1 inn
7-30 (H)	Mariners 4 Cubs 1	Miley 1 Hit 7 inn Daiz 1 Hit 1 inn, Cishek 1 Hit 1 inn.
8-9 (H)	Cubs 5 Angels 1	Lackey 3 Hits 8 inn, Strop 0 Hits 1 inn

1st Game

8-16 (H)	Cubs 4 Brewers 0	Cahill 2 Hits 5 inn, Montgomery 1 Hit 2 inn Rondon 0 Hits 1 inn, Smith 0 Hits ⅓ inn Chapman 0 Hits ⅔ inn
9-1 (H)	Cubs 5 Giants 4	Montgomery 3 Hits 4 inn, Zastryzny 0 Hits 2 inn, Smith 0 Hits 2 inn, Edwards 0 Hits 1 inn
9-2 (H)	Cubs 2 Giants 1	Lester 3 Hits 9 inn
9-7 (A)	Brewers 2 Cubs 1	Garza 3 Hits 6 inn. Torres 0 Hits 1 inn Kuebel 0 Hits 1 inn. Thornburg 0 Hits 1 inn
9-10 (A)	Astros 2 Cubs 1	McHugh 2 Hits 5 inn Devenski 0 Hits 1 inn Harris 0 Hits 1 inn, Gregerson 0 Hits 1 inn Giles 0 Hits 1 inn
9-12 (A)	Cubs 4 Cards 1	Hendricks 1 Hit 8 inn, Chapman 0 Hits 1 inn (1 Hit)
9-14 (A)	Cubs 7 Cards 0	Lester 3 Hits 8 inn, Rondon 0 Hits 1 inn (2 Hits)
9-29 (A)	Cubs 1 Pirates 1	Zastryzyn 3⅔ inn 2 Hits, Wood 0 Hits 1⅔ inn Game stopped after 5 due to weather. Outcome had no effect on standing

29

9th Inning Changes

5-18 (A) Cards 2 Brewers 1	Trailing 1-0 going into the 9th the Cubs tied the score and won it in the 13th
5-23 (A) Cards 4 Cubs 3	Game tied 3 to 3. Cards got a home run in the 9th to win.
6-14 (A) Cubs 4 Nats 3	Tied going into 9th. Cubs get winning run in top of 9th to win
6-15 (A) Nats 5 Cubs 4	Nats ahead into the 9th by one. Rizzo hits a 2 run homer but the Nats tied up in the bottom of the 9th. Cubs score 2 runs in the bottom of the 12th to win the game
6-28 (A) Cubs 7 Reds 2 (15 inn)	The Reds score 1 run to tie the game at 2-2 Cubs win on Baez G.S. in 15th
7-7 (H) Brewers 4 Cubs 3	The Brewers score 1 run to tie the game at 3-3 and win it in the 11st
7-19 (H) Mets 2 Cubs 1	Mets score the winning run with 2 out in the 9th
7-25 (A) W. Sox 5 Cubs 4	Cubs score 1 to tie but lose in bottom of ninth
7-31 (H) Cubs 7 Mariners 6 (12 inn)	Cubs score 3 runs to the game at 6 and 6 win in 12th inn
8-3 (H) Cubs 5 Martins 4	Cubs score 3 runs to win 5-4. The winning run came in on a wild pitch. 2 of the Cubs other runs came in on a bases loaded walk & wild pitch.
8-26 (A) Cubs 6 Dodgers 4	Cubs score 1 run to tie then score 2 to win in 10th
8-29 (H) Cubs 8 Pirates 7	Cubs score 1 run to tie and win in the 13th
9-4 (H) Cubs 3 Giants 2	Cubs score 1 run to tie and win it in the 13th
9-16 (H) Cubs 5 Brewers 4	Cubs score 7 runs to tie and win in the 10th

4-11 (H) Cubs 5 Keds 3   Cubs score 5 runs on 3 Hits
Cubs were being no hit by Finnegan for 6 ⅔ innings and trailed 3-0. Ross singled for the first Cub hit. Szczur hit for Cahill and walked (5th walks for the Cubs). Fowler walked to load the bases. Heywood singled, Ross and Szczur scored. In the 8th Zobrist walked, Soler hit by pitch. Russell homers for 3 runs giving the Cubs a 5-3 win

---

4-15 (H) Rockies 6 Cubs 1
There were 14 hits (10 by the Rockies and 4 by the Cubs,) all singles, The Cubs committed 4 errors, [Hendricks - 1 on a ground ball; Bryant 2 - ground ball, throw; Russell - throw]. Montero had a pass ball.

4-17 (H) Rockies 2 Cubs 0   2 hr's by Arenado were the only runs scored.

4-21 (A) Cubs 6 Reds 0 - Arrieta No Hitter

5-11 (H) Padres 1 Cubs 0 2nd Game. The Padres got only 3 Hits and won the game on a home run. The Cubs got 4 singles. The Padres got 2 singles besides the Home Run. Lackey walked no one and had 7 strikeouts and gave up the 3 hits in 9 innings of work.

5-18 (A) Cubs 2 Brewers 1 13th Inning. Trailing 1-0 going into the 9th The Cubs tied the score. The Brewers had the bases loaded in the 12th with 0 out and didn't score. The Cubs won the game in the 13th on a bases loaded walk.

6-6 (A) Cubs 6 Phillies 4. The Cubs had a 6-0 lead going into the 9th. The relief pitchers gave up a 3 Run Homes, solo Homes, and had the tying run at the plate before the 3rd out was made

---

6-15 (A) Nats 5 Cubs 4
The Cubs are down 1-0 going into the 9th Rizzo 2 run homer in the 9th gives the Cubs a 1 run land but the Nats tie it up in the last of the 9th.

Cubs score 1 run in the 12th but the Nats score 2 runs in the bottom of the 12th to win the game.

8-11 (A) Cubs 4 Cards 3

The Cubs win the game in the 11th Inning on a bases loaded walk

Cubs with 3 or more hits in one Game

4-4 (A) Cubs 9 Angeles 0	Fowler 3 Hits (1 Double)
4-7 (A) Cubs 14 D Backs 6	Rizzo 3 Hits (1 HR, 1 Triple)
	Bryant 3 Hits (1 Double)
4-9 (A) Cubs 4 D'Backs 2	Zorbrist 3 Hits (1 Double)
4-10 (A) Cubs 7 D'Backs 3	La Stella 3 Hits
4-14 (H) Cubs 8 Reds 1	Fowler 3 Hits
	Russell 3 Hits
4-21 (A) Cubs 16 Reds 0	Bryant - 4 Hits (2 HR's - one a grand slam)
	Zobrist - 3 Hits (1 Home Run, 1 Double)
4-24 (A) Cubs 9 Reds 0	La Stella - 3 Hits (1 Home Run, 2 Doubles)
	Heyward - 4 Hits (1 Double)
5-3 (A) Cubs 7 Pirates 1	Bryant - 3 Hits
5-4 (A) Cubs 6 Pirates 2	Rizzo - 3 Hits (Home Runs, Double)
	Baez - 3 Hits
5-5 (H) Cubs 5 Nationals 2	La Stella 3 Hits (1 Double)
5-8 (H) Cubs 4 Nationals 3	Bryant - 3 Hits (Double)
5-10 (H) Cubs 8 Padres 7	Zobrist - 4 Hits
5-13 (H) Cubs 9 Pirates 4	Ross - 3 Hits (Home Run)
5-14 (H) Cubs 8 Pirates 2	Heyward - 3 Hits
5-18 (A) Cubs 2 Brewers 1	
13 Innings	Zobrist - 3 Hits
5-21 (A) Giants 5 Cubs 3	Fowler - 3 Hits (Home Run)
5-23 (A) Cards 4 Cubs 3	Zobrist - 3 Hits
5-24 (A) Cards 12 Cards 3	Fowler - 3 Hits (Double)
5-25 (A) Cubs 9 Cards 8	Zobrist - 3 Hits
6-6 (A) Cubs 6 Phillies 4	Fowler - 3 Hits (Double)
	Bryant - 3 Hits
	Rizzo - 3 Hits
6-8 (A) Cubs 8 Phillies 1	Baez - 4 Hits (Double)

6-11 (A) Cubs 8 Braves 2	Heyward - 3 Hits (Home Run, Double)
6-12 (A) Cubs 13 Braves 2	Rizzo - 3 Hits (Double)
	Heyward - 3 Hits (Double)
6-17 (H) Cubs 6 Pirates 0	Almora - 3 Hits (Double)
6-19 (H) Cubs 10 Pirates 5	Heyward - 3 Hits
	Rizzo - 3 Hits (Home Run)
	Baez - 3 Hits (Home Run)

Cubs with 3 or more Hits in one Game - Cont

6-20 (H) Cards 3 Cubs 2   Zobrist - 3 Hits

6-21 (H) Cards 4 Cubs 3   Russell - 3 Hits (Double)

6-27 (A) Cubs 11 Reds 8   Bryant - 5 Hits (3 Home Runs, 2 Doubles)

6-29 (H) Cubs 9 Reds 2   Baez - 3 Hits (Double)

7-3 (A) Mets 14 Cubs 3   Baez - 3 Hits (Double)

7-7 (H) Brewers 4 Cubs 3   Contreras - 3 Hits (Triple)

7-9 (A) Pirates 12 Cubs 6   Rizzo - 4 Hits (Double Triple)

                                    Heyward - 3 Hits (Double)

7-10 (A) Cubs 6 Pirates 5   Rizzo - 4 Hits (2 Doubles)

                                    Bryant - 3 Hits

7-18 (H) Cubs 5 Mets 1   Szczar - 3 Hits (2 Doubles)

7-20 (H) Cubs 6 Mets 2   Russell - 3 Hits (Double)

7-22 (A) Cubs 5 Brewers 2   Fowler - 3 Hits (Double, Home Run)

7-24 (A) Cubs 6 Brewers 5   La Stella - 3 Hits (Double)

7-25 (A) W. Sox 5 Cubs 4   Baez - 3 Hits (HR, Double)

7-29 (H) Cubs 12 Mariners 1   Bryant - 3 Hits (Double)

                                    Baez - 3 Hits

7-31 (H) Cubs 7 Mariners 6

            12 Inn   Zobrist - 3 Hits (Triple)

8-1 (H) Cubs 5 Marlins 0   Rizzo - 3 Hits (Double, Triple)

8-2 (H) Cubs 3 Marlins 2   Fowler - 3 Hits (Triple)

8-12 (H) Cubs 13 Cards 2   Syczar - 3 Hits (2 HR, 1 Double)

                                    Bryant - 3 Hits (2 Doubles)

8-14 (H) Cards 6 Cubs 4   Rizzo - 3 Hits (Home Run)

8-18 (H) Cubs 9 Brewers 6   Bryant - 5 Hits (2 HR's, Double)

8-20 (A) Cubs 9 Rockies 2   Zobrist - 3 Hits (HR, Double)

                                    Montero - 3 Hits

8-22 (A) Cubs 5 Padres 1   Rizzo - 4 Hits (Double)

8-23 (A) Cubs 5 Padres 3   Zobrist - 3 Hits (Double)

8-29 (A) Cubs 8 Pirates 7   Baez - 4 Hits (Double, Triple)

Soler - 3 Hits (Double, Home Run)

Fowler - 3 Hits

9-4 (H) Cubs 3 Giants 2   Rizzo - 3 Hits

13 Inn   Russell - 3 Hits (2 Doubles)

Heyward - 3 Hits

9-11 (A) Cubs 9 Astros 5   Russell - 3 Hits (Home Run)

3 or More Hits - Cont

9-16 (H) Cubs 5 Brewers 4	Coghlan - 3 Hits (Double)
9-20 (H) Cubs 6 Reds 1	Bryant - 3 Hits (2 Doubles)
9-21 (H) Cubs 9 Reds 2	Zobrist - 3 Hits
	Baez - 3 Hits
	Montero - 3 Hits
9-23 (H) Cubs 5 Cards 0	Rizzo - 3 Hits (2 Doubles)
9-24 (H) Cards 10 Cubs 4	Fowler - 3 Hits (Double, Triple)
9-25 (H) Cubs 3 Cards 1	Zobrist - 3 Hits (Double)
9-26 (H) Cubs 12 Pirates 2	Almora - 3 Hits (Double)
9-30 (A) Cubs 7 Reds 3	Zorbrist - 3 Hits (2 HR's & Double)

Triples

4-7 (A) Cubs 14 D'Backs 6	Fowler, Rizzo
4-26 (H) Cubs 4 Brewers 3	Russell
5-6 (H) Cubs 8 Nationals 6	La Stella
5-7 (H) Cubs 8 Nationals 5	Fowler #2
5-10 (H) Cubs 8 Padres 7	Russell #2
5-19 (A) Brewers 5 Cubs 3	Montero
5-24 (A) Cubs 12 Cards 3	Szczar
5-27 (H) Cubs 6 Phillies 2	Fowler #3
6-24 (A) Cubs 5 Marlins 4	Coghlan
7-7 (H) Brewers 4 Cubs 3	Contreras
7-8 (A) Pirates 8 Cubs 4	Heyward
7-9 (A) Pirates 12 Cubs 6	Rizzo #2
7-22 (A) Cubs 5 Brewers 2	Russell #3
7-31 (H) Cubs 7 Mariners 6	12 Inn Zobrist
8-1 (H) Cubs 5 Marlins 0	Rizzo #3
8-2 (H) Cubs 3 Marlins 2	Fowler #4
8-11 (H) Cubs 4 Cards 3	11-ING Rizzo #4
8-14 (H) Cards 6 Cubs 4	Bryant
8-23 (A) Cubs 5 Padres 3	Arrieta
8-24 (A) Cubs 6 Padres 3	Zobrist #2
8-29 (H) Cubs 8 Pirates 7	13-Inn Baez
8-31 (H) Cubs 6 Pirates 5	Fowler #5
9-9 (A) Cubs 2 Astros 0	Fowler #6
9-14 (A) Cubs 7 Cards 0	Bryant #2
9-17 (H) Brewers 11 Cubs 3	Bryant #3
9-24 (H) Cards 10 Cubs 4	Zobrist #3
9-27 (A) Cubs 6 Pirates 4	Fowler #7
	Coghlan #2
	Almora

Home Runs

4-4 (A) Cubs 9 Angeles 0	Montero - 1 on
4-5 (A) Cubs 6 Angeles 1	Szczur - 0 on
	Rizzo - 1 on
	Fowler - 1 on
4-7 (A) Cubs 14 D'Backs 6	Rizzo - 2 on #2
4-10 (A) Cubs 7 D'Backs 3	Soler - 0 on
	Arrieta - 1 on
4-11 (H) Cubs 5 Reds 3	Russell - 2 on
4-13 (H) Cubs 9 Reds 2	Bryant - 0 on
4-14 (H) Cubs 8 Reds 1	Bryant - 0 on #2
4-16 (H) Cubs 6 Rockies 2	Rizzo - 0 on #3
	Soler - 0 on #2
	Fowler - 2 on #2
4-18 (A) Cubs 5 Cardinals 0	Fowler - 0 on #3
4-21 (A) Cubs 16 Reds 0	Bryant 2 - 1 on #5
	GS #4
	Rizzo - 2 on #5
	Zobrist - 0 on #1
	Ross - 0 on #1
4-22 (A) Cubs 8 Reds 1	Rizzo - 0 on #6
	Baez - 0 on #1
4-23 (A) Reds 13 Cubs 5	Russell - 0 on #2
4-24 (A) Cubs 9 Reds 0	Rizzo - 1 on #7
	Rizzo - 1 on #8
	La Stella 0 on #1
4-28 (H) Cubs 7 Brewers 2	Ross - 0 on #2
4-29 (H) Cubs 6 Braves 1	Szczar - G.S. #2
5-4 (A) Cubs 6 Pirates 2	Zobrist - 2 on #2
	Rizzo - 0 on #9
5-5 (H) Cubs 5 Nationals 2	Zorbrist - 1 on #3

5-6 (H) Cubs 8 Nationals 6	La Stella - 1 on #2
	Rizzo - 0 on #10
	Zobrist 2 - 0 on #4, 2 on #5
5-7 (H) Cubs 8 Nationals 5	Bryant - 0 on #5
5-8 (H) Cubs 4 Nationals 3	Baez - 0 on #2
5-13 (H) Cubs 9 Pirates 4	Russell - 2 on #3
	Bryant - 1 on #6
	Ross - 2 on #3
5-14 (H) Cubs 8 Pirates 2	Rizzo 2 on #11
	Russell 1 on #4

Home Runs

5-17 (A) Brewers 4 Cubs 2	Heyward	0 on #1
	Bryant	0 on #7
5-19 (A) Brewers 5 Cubs 3	Fowler	0 on #4
5-20 (A) Cubs 8 Giants 1	Bryant	2 on #8
	Zorbrist	0 on #6
	Soler	0 on #3
5-21 (A) Giants 5 Cubs 3	Fowler	0 on #5
	Bryant	0 on #9
5-24 (A) Cubs 12 Cards 3	Soler	1 on #4
5-25 (A) Cubs 9 Cards 8	Bryant	2 on #10
5-27 (H) Cubs 6 Phillies 2	Soler	0 on #5
	Ross	2 on #4
	Bryant	0 on #11
5-28 (H) Cubs 4 Phillies 1	Fowler	0 on #6
5-29 (H) Cubs 7 Phillies 2	Montero	0 on #2
	Zobrist	2 on #7
6-1 (H) Cubs 2 Dodgers 1	Bryant	1 on #12
6-2 (H) Cubs 7 Dodgers 2	Baez	1 on #3
	Heyward	0 on #2
	Bryant	0 on #13
	Rizzo	0 on #12
6-4 (H) Cubs 5 D'Backs 3	Fowler	0 on #7
	Rizzo	0 on #13
6-5 (H) D'Backs 3 Cubs 2	Baez	0 on #4
6-6 (A) Cubs 6 Phillies 4	Heyward	1 on #3
6-8 (A) Cubs 8 Phillies 1	Bryant	1 on #14
	Zobrist	0 on #8

6-11 (A) Cubs 8 Braves 2	Heyward	0 on #4
	Rizzo	0 on #14
	Bryant	1 on #15
	Montero	2 on #3
6-12 (A) Cubs 13 Braves 2	Baez	2 on #5
6-13 (A) Nats 4 Cubs 1	Russell	0 on #5
6-15 (A) Nats 5 Cubs 4	Zobrist	0 on #9
	Rizzo	1 on #15
6-17 (H) Cubs 6 Pirates 0	Szczur	1 on #3
6-18 (H) Cubs 4 Pirates 3	Rizzo	0 on #16
	Bryant	0 on #16

Home Runs - Cont

6-18 (H) Cubs 4 Pirates 3	Ross 0 on #5
6-19 (H) Cubs 10 Pirates 5	Baez 0 on #6
	Bryant 0 on #17
	Rizzo 0 on #17
	Contreras 1 on #1
	Russell 1 on #6
6-22 (H) Cards 7 Cubs 2	Contreras 1 on #2
6-23 (A) Marlins 4 Cubs 2	Ross 0 on #6
6-24 (A) Cubs 5 Marlins 4	Bryant 0 on #18
	Contreras 1 on #3
6-25 (A) Marlins 9 Cubs 6	Montero 0 on #4
	Russell 2 on #7
6-27 (A) Cubs 11 Reds 8	3 Bryant 0 on, 2 on, 0 on #21
	Rizzo 0 on #18
	Arrieta 0 on #2
6-28 (A) Cubs 7 Reds 2 15 inn	Zobrist 0 on #10
	Baez 3 on #7 G. S.
6-29 (A) Cubs 9 Reds 2	Rizzo 2 on #19
	Russell 0 on #8
	Almora 0 on #1
6-30 (A) Mets 4 Cubs 3	Bryant 1 on #22
	Baez 0 on #8
7-1 (A) Mets 10 Cubs 2	Bryant 0 on #23
7-2 (A) Mets 4 Cubs 3	Rizzo 1 on #20
	Zobrist 0 on #11
7-3 (A) Mets 14 Cubs 3	Contreras 0 on #4
7-4 (H) Cubs 10 Reds 4	Bryant 1 on #24
	Contreras 0 on #5
	Russell 1 on #9

7-5 (H) Reds 9 Cubs 5

Baez 0 on #9

Bryant 0 on #25

2 Russell 1 on #10, 0 on #11

7-6 (H) Reds 5 Cubs 3

Zobrist 0 on #12

7-7 (A) Pirates 8 Cubs 4

Montero 1 on #5

Rizzo - 0 on #21

7-9 (A) Pirates 12 Cubs 6

Zobrist 1 on #13

7-10 (A) Cubs 6 Pirates 5

Almora 1 on #2

7-18 (H) Cubs 5 Mets 1

Rizzo 2 on #22

7-20 (H) Cubs 6 Mets 2

2 Rizzo 0 on #23, 1 on #24

Home Runs - Cont

7-22 (A) Cubs 5 Brewers 2	Fowler - 0 on #8
7-25 (A) W. Sox 5 Cubs 4	Baez 1 on #10
7-27 (H) Cubs 8 W. Sox 1	Bryant 0 on #26
	Baez 1 on #11
	Russell - G. S. #12
7-29 (H) Cubs (2 Mariners)	Heyward 1 on #5
	Ross 0 on #7
8-5 (A) Cubs 7 A's 2	Fowler 0 on #9
	Soler 2 on #6
8-7 (A) Cubs 3 A's 1	Bryant 0 on #27
	Soler 0 on #7
8-9 (H) Cubs 5 Angels 1	Contreras 0 on #6
	Bryant 0 on #28
8-10 (H) Cubs 3 Angels 1	Russell 0 on #13
8-12 (H) Cubs 13 Cards 2	Contreras 2 on #7
	2 Szczur 0 on #4, 1 on #5
	Soler 0 on #8
	Baez 1 on #12
8-13 (H) Cards 8 Cubs 4	Russell 1 on #14
8-14 (H) Cards 6 Cubs 4	Rizzo 0 on #25
8-16 (H) Cubs 4 Brewers 1	Baez 1 on #13

2nd Game

8-17 (H) Cubs 6 Brewers 1	Soler 2 on #9
	Ross 0 on #8
8-18 (H) Cubs 9 Brewers 6	2 Bryant 1 on #29, 0 on #30
8-19 (A) Rockies 7 Cubs 6 11 inn	Fowler 0 on #10
	Russell 1 on #15
8-20 (A) Cubs 9 Rockies 2	Bryant 2 on #31
	Zorbrist 0 on #14

8-21 (A) Rockies 11 Cubs 4   2 Russell 0 on #16, 0 on #17

8-22 (A) Cubs 5 Padres 1   Russell 0 on #18

Bryant 0 on #32

Heyward 1 on #6

8-23 (A) Cubs 5 Padres 3   Bryant 0 on #33

Russell 1 on #19

8-24 (A) Cubs 6 Padres 3   Contreras 0 on #8

8-26 (A) Cubs 6 Dodgers 4   2-Bryant 0 on #34, 1 on #35

8-29 (H) Cubs 8 Pirates 7 13 inn   Contreras 1 on #9

Soler 0 on #10

8-30 (H) Cubs 3 Pirates 0   Rizzo 1 on #26

8-31 (H) Cubs 6 Pirates 5   Bryant 0 on #36

9-6 (A) Brewers 12 Cubs 5   2 Rizzo 0 on #27, 1 on #28

9-7 (A) Brewers 2 Cubs 1   Rizzo 0 on #29

9-9 (A) Cubs 2 Astros 0   Bryant 1 on #37

9-11 (A) Cubs 9 Astros 5   Soler 0 on #11

Russell 1 on #20

9-12 (A) Cubs 4 Cards 1   Zorbrist 0 on #15

Fowler 1 on #11

9-13 (A) Cards 4 Cubs 2   Fowler 0 on #12

9-14 (A) Cubs 7 Cards 0   Ross 1 on #9

2 Rizzo 0 on #30, 1 on #31

9-15 (H) Brewers 5 Cubs 4   Soler 1 on #12

9-16 (H) Cubs 5 Brewers 4   Almora 1 on #3

Montero 0 on #7

9-17 (H) Brewers 11 Cubs 3   Coghlan 1 on #1

9-19 (H) Cubs 5 Reds 2   Russell 0 on #21

Heyward 1 on #7

Contreras 0 on #10

9-21 (H) Cubs 9 Reds 2   Fowler 0 on #13

Bryant 1 on #38

9-24 (H) Cards 10 Cubs 4   Contreras 0 on #11

9-25 (H) Cubs 3 Cards 1   Ross 0 on #10

9-26 (A) Cubs 12 Pirates 2   Baez 3 on #14 G. S.

     Bryant 1 on #39

9-28 (A) Pirates 8 Cubs 4   Rizzo 0 on #32

9-30 (A) Cubs 7 Reds 3   2 Zorbrist - 0 on & 1 on #17

10-1 (A) Cards 7 Cubs 4   Zorbrist 0 on #18

10-2 (A) Cubs 7 Red 4   Contreras 0 on #12

     Montero 1 on #8

2016 Cub Awards for Regular Season

National League MVP - Kris Bryant
National League Silver Slugger - Anthony Rizzo for First Basemen
    "   "   "   "   Jake Arrieta for pitchers
National League Gold Gloves - Anthony Rizzo for First Basemen
    "   "   "   "   Jason Howard for Right Field
National League Platinum Glove - Anthony Rizzo
      (Best defenseman)

Extra Innings 9-W 4-L

5-8 (H)	Cubs 4 Nationals 3	13 INNINGS
5-18 (A)	Cubs 2 Brewers 1	13 INNINGS
5-1 (H)	Braves 4 Cubs 3	10 INNINGS
6-15 (A)	Nationals 5 Cubs 4	12 INNINGS
6-28 (A)	Cubs 7 Reds 2	15 INNINGS
7-7 (H)	Braves 4 Cubs 3	11 INNINGS
7-31 (H)	Cubs 7 Mariners 6	12 INNINGS
8-11 (H)	Cubs 4 Cards 3	11 INNINGS
8-19 (A)	Rockies 7 Cubs 6	11 INNINGS
8-26 (A)	Cubs 6 Dodgers 4	10 INNINGS
8-29 (H)	Cubs 8 Pirates 7	13 INNINGS
9-4 (H)	Cubs 3 Giants 2	13 INNINGS
9-16 (H)	Cubs 5 Brewers 4	10 INNINGS

Comparing the 2015 & 2016 Cubs

	2015	2016
Shutouts	W-17 L-6	W-15 L-6
9th Inning Charges	W-13 L-4	W-9 L-5
Pitchers Giving Up 3 or less Hits	W-12 L-6	W-21 L-10
Extra Innings	W-13 L-5	W-9 L-4
Double Headers	W-2 9-7	W-1 8-16
	9-11	
	L-0	L-1 5-11
	Split 2 7-22	
	9-15	Split - 0

Wins and Losses by Month
(57 HOME GAME WINS RECORD)

April	12-W 8-L 2-RAIN	17-W 5-L 2-RAIN
May	14-W 14-L 1-RAIN	18-W 10-L 1-RAIN
June	14-W 13-L 1 RAIN	16-W 12-L
July	15-W 12-L	12 W 14-L
Aug	19-W 9-L 1 RAIN	22-W 6-L
Sept	19-W 9-L	17-W 10-L 1-TIE
Oct	4-W 0-L	1-W 1-L
	97 65	103 58 1 TIE

Playoff Games

The 25 players that played in the playoff games are as follows:

11 Pitchers

Jake Arrieta, Aroldis Chapman, Carl Edwards Jr., Justin Grimm, Kyle Hendricks, John Lackey Jon Lester, Mike Montgomery, Hector Rondon, Pedro Strop, Travis Wood, Rob Zastryzny (1)

3 Catchers

Wilson Contreras, Miguel Montero, David Ross

6 Infielders

Javier Baez, Kris Bryant, Tommy La Stella (2) Anthony Rizzo, Addison Russell, Ben Zobrist

5 Outfielders

Albert Almore Jr., Chris Coghlan, Dexter Fowler Jason Heyward, Kyle Schwarber (3), Jorge Soler

- (1) Played only in the N.L. Championship Game
- (2) Played only in the N.L. Divisional Game
- (3) Played only in the World Series

National League Divisional Games (Best 3 of 5 Games)

Game 1 (10-7-16) (H) Cubs 1 Giants 0
Game 2 (10-8-16) (H) Cubs 5 Giants 2
Game 3 (10-10-16) (A) Giants 6 Cubs 5 13 innings
Game 4 (10-11-16) (A) Cubs 6 Giants 5

National League Championship Games (Best 4 of 7 Games)

Game 1 (10-15-16) (H) Cubs 8 Dodgers 4
Game 2 (10-16-16) (H) Dodgers 1 Cubs 0
Game 3 (10-18-16) (A) Dodgers 6 Cubs 0
Game 4 (10-19-16) (A) Cubs 10 Dodgers 2
Game 5 (10-20-16) (A) Cubs 8 Dodgers 4
Game 6 (10-22-16) (H) Cubs 5 Dodgers 0
MVP –Javier Baez

World Series (Best 4 of 7 Games)

Game 1 (10-25-16) (A) Cleveland 6 Cubs 0
Game 2 (10-26-16) (A) Cubs 5 Cleveland 1
Game 3 (10-28-16) (A) Cleveland 1 Cubs 0
Game 4 (10-29-16) (H) Cleveland 7 Cubs 2
Game 5 (10-30-16) (H) Cubs 3 Cleveland 2
Game 6 (11-1-16) (A) Cubs 9 Cleveland 3
Game 7 (11-2-16) (A) Cubs 8 Cleveland 7   10 Innings

Cubs win 1st world series after 108 years.

World Series MVP - Ben Zorbrist

CUBS WIN 1ST WORLD SERIES AFTER 108 YEARS!

Printed in the United States
By Bookmasters